Take Life By the Throat
by

TW Williams

Published by TW WILLIAMS

ISBN: 978-1-7323168-1-2

Copyright © 2018 by TW WILLIAMS

Discover other titles by TW WILLIAMS at http://timwms.com

This book is a work of poetry. Names, characters, places and incidents either are products of the poet's imagination or are used fictitiously. Any resemblance to actual events or locales or persons, living or dead, is entirely coincidental.

All rights reserved, including the right of reproduction in whole or in part in any form.

Acknowledgements

"Long Walk to Camp", *Joyful! Online*, 2010

"Her Callipygian Behind", *Writer's Digest*, 10th Place, 6th Poetry Competition, 2010

"Missy Elli's Travails", *SP Quill Magazine*, November 2010

"Fire Frozen", *Diverse Voices Quarterly,* October 2010

"Life Changes", *SP Quill Magazine*, May 2009

"Water Wealth", *SP Quill Magazine*, May 2009

"Aspen Grove Chorales", *The Griffin*, April 2012

"Glass Singing", *The Alembic*, March 2011

"Norwegian and Ponderosa Pines", *The Griffin*, April 2012

"Next Time We Will Be Kinder", *A Word Is Worth a Thousand Pictures, An Anthology of Poetry,* edited by Domenik Lopane, 2011

"Relentless Changes", *The Griffin*, April 2012

"Won't Catch Me," *The Dos Passos Review, 2014*

TABLE OF CONTENTS

ACKNOWLEDGEMENTS

HER CALLIPYGIAN BEHIND

SOMEWHAT CROSS

GLASS SINGING

LONG WALK TO CAMP

PHOTONS

SHE SETS IN THE WEST

NEVER MINE

FLAMES TURN TO ASH

FIRE FROZEN

DELICIOUS FATE

TUNNELS

NEXT LIFETIME WE WILL BE KINDER

DECK MASTER

BACKYARD ADVENTURES

KITE MAN RIDES A CHARIOT

WON'T CATCH ME

COFFEE DREAMS

JAMES DEAN

RELENTLESS CHANGES

SCENT

NORWEGIAN AND PONDEROSA PINES

ASPEN GROVE CHORALES

DECEPTION
FALL SMELL
WATER WEALTH
LETTER TO MY FAMILY
HOSPITAL BLUES
MISSY ELLI'S COMEBACK
BUSY FLOATING, THANK YOU
TIME MACHINE
SIX BILLION YEARS
RENDERER
NEW FLOWER
CASUAL CHOICE

HER CALLIPYGIAN BEHIND

They say she is a plain gal
who attracts many a guy
thus, they accuse her
of pagan wiles, but
really, it's perfectly
portioned buttocks,
her callipygian behind,
that bounces below her iliac
that sways gaily and galls
town ladies who feel
she's plying wares
but men hearing
their whining sigh
wonder what artist
sculpted her hips out
of Elysian clay.

SOMEWHAT CROSS

He walked
upon earth
God's gift
Wanted to
show love
from God was limitless, boundless
not just vengeance, war, and hate
of those fools who did not follow
Him like those usurious Hypocrites
Paul came,
organized
doctrines
of Church
Wonder if
Christ sits
in Heaven
inquiring
where all
the Gentiles
came from.

GLASS SINGING

a note clear and pure
rings off crystal
glass as my
wet finger
spins
round,
round.
Lands
upon
ears
pristine. Lures me
like a siren to Ulysses
to join her in ecstasy.

MY BALLOON TUGS AT ME

Hundreds of voices rise and fall,
bodies move, in, out, all about.
I stare at the clown
holding a hundred balloons
who, walking on his toes,
nearly floats.

He spies me, small, astounded,
grins widely with fat red lips,
winks, pulls one out for me:
a blue balloon of Earth
with lands so strange.

An airplane flies
across untroubled skies,
a train runs over bridges,
mountains, plains.
A ship courses
atop placid ocean
to a sunny beach
with a giant coconut tree.

I feel lighter,
my balloon tugs at me,
soon we will fly.

LONG WALK TO CAMP

The walk on the road to camp
was so long for a little boy
who spied Indians hiding behind
wrinkled grey tree trunks.
Cowboys in chaps, spurs,
cap guns cocked
tipped their hats to him
from across the stream.
Fauns waited with smiles
behind mounds, fallen trees.
All in the weald
down the bank.

Creek water pure and clear
rippled musical notes
over cleansing rocks.
Pebbles round,
colored clay-red,
yellow-white
distorted by swirling currents
winked up
at his curious eyes.

Sun rays cooked green leaves,
fern fronds bathed in hot moist air
suspended beneath dark-green canopies.
Acrid earthy odors of loam
interlaced with aromas
of decayed brown leaves
lured, tugged at him
to turn, to enter.

A green truck slowly drew near.
Moans, groans, creaking, aching springs,
became shrieks, screams as it rumbled by.
He waved to the rider in the cab
high above dust and fumes,
who only stared ahead.
The boy turned
to find the forest
somber, quiet.

PHOTONS

photons,
are they some wave,
some particle, some threads
used to weave the universe's tale?
just light

A JEWEL WEARS MY SOUL

Our star cuts an arc across blue sky as our planet spins,
her smile attracts desire, my mind opens artesian spring.

Jimma spreads chaotically with Italian mansions, lowly huts,
merchant stores merge, people mingle at markets, tin roofs gleam.

Dogs fight, burros bear burdens, men laugh, women scold
wandering bare children, lorries rumble, dust rises above din.

A jewel walks by as if dangling on spun gold thread,
mesmerized I stumble, stutter, pursue its glitter.

Dancers rush onto floor, singers greet joined couples,
crowds yell, clap to beat, shoulders shake the *skesta*.

Youngsters gyrate, imitate, teen age girls giggle
at outlander's tongue fumbling to ask for one dance.

Mother hands on hips directs pounding of wheat grain
shakes her finger for dropping water on thirsty dust.

A jet lands in New York City where gated portals
allow the jewel to wear my soul upon her shiny chest.

SHE FLOWS ACROSS THE DANCE FLOOR OUT OF THE DARK

She flows across the dance floor out of the dark
Layered smoke yields, swirls around her gliding form
to light fire in my eyes and love to last.

I forget past timid questions posed to painted dolls
cross her path to catch her smile, drink her scent.
She flows across the dance floor out of the dark.

Her hand is soft, unafraid, lips spread in red.
She flows across the dance floor out of the dark
to light fire in my eyes and love to last.

Music plays to deaf ears, our minds flood,
our bodies mirror melody in our sways and dips.
She flows across the dance floor out of the dark

SHE SETS IN THE WEST

Her hair is dark as raven feathers at night,
cascades along cheeks to back.
Saunters by with proud gait
as her black patterned stitched boots

crunch pumice, dirt. Blue jean clad hips
sway, orbs bounce softly
beneath pearl-buttoned pockets
of her western blouse. The earth wobbles.

She's a mysterious force
of invisible, powerful waves
that repel, attract me. At her whim
she artfully stretches me out.

I bob like a buoy before her,
head just above water, able only to stare
into those deep impenetrable irises,
soft as black velvet evening gowns.

It's wretched to live on another world
when so young, so trapped by gravity.
Hundreds of miles from her are as remote
as light years between shimmering stars.

Time, distance, choice conspire
to decimate desires of deeper bonds
blast them into orbits as disparate
as boiling Mercury is from frozen Pluto.

I rise in the east, she sets in the west.
Sometimes memories present her
as the changed face of a pale moon
that visits a day's clear blue sky.

I stare at her faded aspect, understand
as inevitably as captured meteorites,
we shall each burn like bright lights
as we plummet into our last nights.

NEVER MINE

Milky Way's river of billions flows across black sky
her soft lips carry me, golden curls creep around my face.

Oklahoma City cut into precise squares of grass by class,
mothers feed daughters' myths of white cascading dreams.

Creek gurgles behind the cabin, waves of wind conduct
branches to lead songs moaned from rustling needles, aspen leaves.

My hand caresses a firm thigh that will never be mine,
softness will come and grow while I wander woods of pine.

Embers of a roaring campfire fight to keep flames,
avoid becoming ash while men pour water, delight in their hiss.

Boys and girls whisper the night into dark, dreamy sleep,
my arms hold onto a ghost dissolving into clouding memory.

She plots and schemes best for her, leaves pack the ground
until not one blade of grass grows, even in spring.

FLAMES TURN TO ASH

Flaming fingers claw at stars
greedily consume air above,
leap for sky, fall short.
She and I nearby lie
at the end ecstatically scream
wonder if we made
dreams real together.

Blue-yellow light
spreads warmth
to our flagging bodies.
Fleeting moments
flicker and flare
in my mind's eye.
Smoke gathers,
pine wood crackles,
thirsty red tongues rise, falter.

One log in our campfire breaks,
one collapses, sparks fly, die.
Logs transform
to white-hot embers,
sputter, sparkle.
Warmth recedes,
vision darkens.

Her eyes close,
mine blink,
sting with tears.
We briefly burn,
crumble into the night.

FIRE FROZEN

Abrupt loss
smears scenes.
He rewinds
hazy film
to regret
their last scene
amid angry words.

Need to see her face,
touch her breast,
smell her
left him a beggar
too emaciated
to lift his hand
for food or coin.

Fickle gods caused
their meeting, melding,
doomed one to sleep
the other to walk
trodden paths.
Sculpted memory
paints his fire frozen.

DELICIOUS FATE

***Inspired by "The Lady and the Tiger"
by Frank Stockton***

The tiger paces to and fro.
Its stripes flash between bars
of its cage. It pauses,
stretches its claws,
looks hungrily at me
with merciless yellow eyes.
Gorgeous growls shake my will.

Will I let him slash, devour
my lover? The kill
with any other would be
as sweet as when honey drips,
pools from a raised spoon.
He is mine! Mine alone.

My sire desires
he be tested, choose
death or life.
Life with whore
of our court, or death
from this beast.
My king plays with us,
plays to see Fate's course.

Two doors inside the ring:
one to horrid fate,
or one too horrid.
How can I bear them?
Both bound for life,
exiled from me.
Not to touch him,

not to be with him,
not him in me, on me.

I am princess,
I am precious to all,
I am a wonder.
But only he is beautiful,
only he breaks my heart,
splits my mind apart.

He should not die.
He should not live
for any but this heart,
this heart pumping rage,
aching with fear.

Tomorrow my pet
you will make my choice yours.
Your fate hangs
like a dog fixated
on a bone out of reach.
Your pulse will stop.
Your eyes will gaze
upon this soft fingertip
with polished, sharpened nail
as it points.
Which door will it be?

TUNNELS

tunnels
built to pierce deeply
mountain veins, its muscle
so man can pass in a straight line
heavy

NEXT LIFETIME WE WILL BE KINDER

So that we can casually meander
cobblestone sidewalks in slow procession,
hands locked behind our backs,
smile to one another, gasp mild surprises

So that without demands of attention
or obsessions become easy friends,
have conversations no matter
where we might roam day or night.

Today, we duel with honed foils.
dense clouds darken felicity's doorway.
Once a tapestry interwoven with magic
we have unraveled into piles of twine.

Should alternate universes exist,
could we experience meaningful meetings,
or would diurnal tides' repetitive rhythm
vie to cast us once more on opposite shores?

DECK MASTER

I relish this time alone
on my deck as I grill.
My lover conjures salads
in the kitchen.
I am Master of Fire and Spit
I watch flames lick
at chicken leg skins, burgers sizzle
from mottled red to brown.
I twirl batons
of spatula, knife,
conduct nature's marvelous concertos
of motion, sound.
Birds croon warbling tunes from swaying trees
while wind waltzes circles in my hair.

Ideas embark from ports
on my mind's river
with beckoning beacons,
beg to unload bags of their seeds
onto furrowed fields to germinate
in rich, black earth.
Dreams grow into shape,
dangle just beyond grasp.
Time drips by like grease off grill's edge.
I feel fresh, free.
Chicken legs are hot, spicy,
hamburgers grilled just right.
She brings me a wide-open tray.
I place a succulent morsel
into her mouth.

LIFE CHANGES

Watches
tick life away
or maybe they show change
of life from beginning
to end
in time

BACKYARD ADVENTURES

I.

One humid day
in our backyard
I ran to the deep shade
of tall black cherry trees
with whorled dark bark,
filled with plump fruit
standing like English guards
tolerating my eager climbs,
sure swings to their crowns
far above ground
where perched
in a forked, crooked
crow's nest
I surveyed the ocean
watched, waited
for the new or dangerous
while sea wind's flow
rocked me back, forth, around.

II.

My little brother,
faithful first mate,
and I, Captain Blood,
leapt from lower roof
of our garage
onto warped dried deck
of Long John's rickety
skull and bones ship.
Ah, the slaughter,
the mauling of men
who did not bleed

was massive.
We saved mankind
repeatedly until
finally, the sheriff,
alias "The Admiral",
arrested us for sake of his roof.

III.

On suspended sentence,
exiled from my brother,
I put on clean clothes,
coonskin hat,
my brand-new leather shoes
to wander among stalwart friends,
the Giant Ancient Barked Ones,
in forests far beyond my backyard
hunting for, exploring new lands,
rivers Daniel Boone
had never found.

I discovered
a small gurgling creek
where I chased frogs,
tried to catch fish
with my hands,
built a dam packed
with leaves, pebbles,
dark brown mud,
changed water's natural course.
A tiny god playing
in a humongous universe.

The sun crept down
my friends' spines.
My feet turned cold,
my hands looked
like giant prunes.
I returned to my backyard
where the stern Lawmaker,
arms crossed, toes tapping
blew out her eyeballs,
screamed, pointed
at my ruined, brand-new shoes.

More days,
more adventures to come.

I AM BATMAN BECAUSE I CANNOT FLY

I stand next
to our home's
gray-stoned wall,
wonder why tall men
with white hardhats
look through spyglasses
like Captain Kid's, who scour
the sea's horizon
for heavily laden ships
to ransom or plunder.
These pirates drive
sharp, wooden stakes
with mysterious numbers
and red-colored flag strips
into hallowed ground.
I pull out their markers,
throw them
into a wet,
dirty ditch.

Why must the Rosenthals leave
their trimmed, perfect yard,
leave the full weeping willow
with sweeping branches
that pet the grass blades
when breezes blow?
Why must they abandon
flower gardens
of tulips, roses, daisies
that splash a ten acre
green canvas with red,
yellow, white life? What will
red-faced, white-haired Pop
do without his tractor
to cruise?

I spy trees
of the old forest
across the street
standing proud
with tall trunks
puffed out
until their bark cracks.
In thanks,
they gently wave to me
with noble grace.
Pop points
at dark thunderheads
with his chin
while I realize
I have saved all of us,
a hero forever,
know that bulldozers,
dump trucks will crumble
to rust and dust.

I am Batman because I cannot fly.

KITE MAN RIDES A CHARIOT

Ocean storm blows, billows
blue, yellow rectangular silk taut,
pulls a small wiry man hard
mocking his arms' strength
yanking them back, forth
up, down, around.

Hidden in his backpack
resides a pulley of ropes
to control kite, resist escape.
His feet bounce across dunes
skimming short streaks,
spaces left where he leaps
as if sending Morse code
to gray pillowed sky above.

Baseball hat screwed on tight,
sunglasses tied tight behind head
he struggles, endures power
of suffering silk, fights
to tame small soaring slice
of nature's raw force.

Behind him cart waits
to churn down coast. He moves
reluctant kite
from vertical to horizontal,
sits in chariot, wind draws
him away
like Apollo's Helios.

WON'T CATCH ME

Won't catch me at the diner any more,
hash browns might as well be fried in vinegar,
radiation destroyed my sense of smell,
I no longer detect wafts of rich black coffee.

Not going to see me at the mall's cinema
where killer agent VX can be a glowing green ball,
or Vin Diesel flies down a thousand-foot cliff
to drive off with tens of millions, chicks.

No one will espy me with gaping mouth,
glazed eyes lapping up TV's high frequency waves
trying to maim my brain so I hate my fellow man
or blame hard working brown people for woes.

No, none of that. My son sits upon mantel
draped in medals, my wife perpetually smiles –
hopefully at me. Grandchildren visit,
run around me on whirlpool's edge.

COFFEE DREAMS

One clean morning
we sit by bay window
view clear blue sky, fresh, crispy.
Waving, yearning colored leaves strain
are swept away in brisk fall fashion.

Our coffee smells of earth,
faraway lands' bright red beans
picked from green trees
on cool high plateaus
strewn to dry on latticed straw mats.

Poor farmers lament
flow of brown gold
through calloused fingers
into sweaty soft palms
of crass, greedy courtiers
of Mammon.

We sit to relax,
to forget, to taste terrestrial brew
of wind, rain, sun.

We entreat our horrid deeds
to fade in vapors.
We ache
to break cured crusts
atop our dreams,
to heal, to feel
our hearts beat.

JAMES DEAN

James Byron Dean
worshiped star of screen,
loved to race and speed
ended up killed by a Turnupseed.

RELENTLESS CHANGES

Colors change hues
that roll up and down
valley and hill
in a relentless march,
in a gaily repetitive annual plan.

A cacophony of crisp winds
carry tunes of panic
among Pan's pagan pals
who blow their last hurried notes
before the icy breezes come.

Trees release leaves
for winter's arrival,
yet some refuse the calling
cling on branch tips,
doggedly lag behind.

Their skeletons lie on the ground
await strong gales to sweep
them away to a rotting, restful place
where they nurture soil,
fertilize future life.

SCENT

scent
awakes
sleeping mind
grandma's biscuits
steam, wait for butter
to melt, golden honey
to pool in crannies and holes
one Tennessee August morning
uncle Bob persuades me Angus cows
give us sweet delicious chocolate milk

NORWEGIAN AND PONDEROSA PINES

I gaze at my Norwegian pines,
my still spindly nude Red Maple,
hear loud melodies sung by robins.
Yard grass flattens on muddy ground
melting from winter snows, rains,
detect green eager to burst out.

Yet I glimpse once again
another point in time
riding on serpentine trail
crawling up to mountain top.
I smell sweat from horses,
boys, men, girls, resins
from Ponderosa pines, hear
creaking crackles of leather
from polished saddles,
realize I am stuck behind a gelding
nowhere to go but straight, helpless
as it unloads onto the trail.

My senses tingle
at bucolic scenes I realize
may be forgotten or turn fuzzy
while I envision sights, sounds, smells
played before man reached the moon.

ASPEN GROVE CHORALES

From one
grows a grove
of clones to rise up,
to worship aloud
under warm, golden beams.

Slender silvery lean trunks
assemble upon meadow floors
like church choirs
upon tiered stages
preparing to sing.

Green leaves swivel
in frenzied clapping circles,
raising vocal harmonies
around elemental melodies
whenever mountain winds
cascade through valley.

If not us,
who would feel
breezy turmoil tearing
through spindly branches,
hear their chorales, witness
their frantic leaves gesturing
wildly like thousands of hands
waving, pleading for attention?

FOREVER IN FLIGHT

We never portray her flecked face the same
Those gray blemishes move from side to side,
Her visage casts argent beam onto earth
Where shadows revolve and stretch to cover

The streams and mountains revealed during day
Unless clouds draw across as blinds a window
Or phases change from crescent, half to full
Or hides from us to enter a new stage.

But her inconstant states remain unchanged
f observed with measured and studied stare
She lives to set or glow each night, orbits
In passing, never idle, a hostage.

DECEPTION

"You can't trust water - even a straight stick turns crooked in it."
W. C. Fields

In deserts travelers see sky
as if placid lakes. Rays bend
below horizon, images flip --
in Antarctica, prone mountains spike up.

Ocean's pink sunset artificially generated
from industrial aerosols transforms colors
as deftly as an artist at his easel –
it's grand to view nature at its best.

Some creeks, rivers flow crystal clear
inviting visitors, but their hosts are dead
from heavy metals, acids trickled
from gaping wounds in mountainsides.

Mr. Fields preferred whiskey to water –
he knew his drink

FALL SMELL

. . . Smell . . .
fallen brown, yellow, red leaves
rotting with the taste of death
in morning's cool, moist air
that penetrates to the marrow.

WATER WEALTH

Water
two molecules
hydrogen oxygen
give life and wealth
to those who
have wells

LETTER TO MY FAMILY

[Inspired by a letter from miner who was killed in the Upper Bridge Massey coal mine disaster (2010) to his wife and kids. He wrote the letter just prior to his death].

I. Letter

My darling, I am dead
though I walk in our home
through living room, den,
though I watch TV
with you and the kids.
Even now, when I play
with Judy and George,
I can't draw a full breath,
black spit comes from my chest,
my nose, throat.
Like a zombie my feet
are heavy, slap thuds
on ground and floor.

Boss told me not to talk
about the top not shored,
dust so thick, so dark
lights cannot shine through,
not to whine about methane gas
or about no ventilation
to clear gas out, give us air.
If I, or anyone else, does
we will be fired. How
can I pay Judy's doctor bills?
Buy her those shots she needs?
Remember me, my darling.

II. 10 Days Later

My darling, I am dead
or soon will be. I can't move.
Blast threw me against wall,
cracked my hard hat
like a walnut shell
tween my finger and thumb,
fell in this heap at its foot.
I have lost the little breath
I could get. I see nothing.
So dark I do not know
if I have lost my sight.
Tell George life is in the air
above the black ground.

HOSPITAL BLUES

Save me from all this pain,
weakness, nausea, fevers,
these chills, night sweats.
My back has exquisite pain,
I can't sit, stand long,
just barely walk. I struggle
to put one foot in front of other.

Save me from all this pain.
Nurse, give me a magic bullet,
make it go away, way yonder,
a pill to melt the hurt
so it pours through my feet
into dark, brown dirt below.

Save me from all this pain.
I room with a man
who whines he can't sleep
so they give him sleeping pills,
a small screen TV that plays
war movies until midnight.
He sleeps sucking air, gurgling
while I burn bonfires
on my forehead and ice cubes
rattle inside my shaking chest.

Save me from all this pain.
In the hospital, I meet my doctors
who gravely stare, give nurses
my free tickets and rides
to MRI, X-Ray, Imaging rooms,
several invasive procedures.
Not sure I want to ride
in their amusement park.

Save me from all this pain, doctors!
"Sir", an Indian doc said,
"You have infections
in your blood and back!"
So steady her brown-eyed gaze,
I guess she never smiled,
else her cheeks might crack
into shards of clay.

Gave me my own room,
My hospital bed felt
like it would take off, orbit.
It went up and down,
blew air in and out all day long
unless I lay still, didn't move.
If I rolled over, I travelled
several light-years.

Save me from all this pain.
Pleasant nurses come
to get my vitals at all times
of day and night. I mumble
and grumble and whoosh!
they leave, but many come back
fill their vials, bottles
with my dark red blood.

Save me from this pain, doctor.
"I can't allow you to leave."
What? I am better. need to go.
"Yes, but your blood must be negative."
Negative, negative is bad isn't it? "No,
negative is good, means clean."
Should be positive, you know,
only in labs does positive mean bad.

Most of my pain has left.
Home at last. Can't sleep.
Miss unexpected guests,
vampires in middle of night.
Long for space travel.

MISSY ELLI'S COMEBACK

Missy Elli lies in wait on layered
succulent green leaves; soon teeth crunch her.
Swallowed, she's dipped into acid,
survives keen enzymes, gut squeeze
still, beat, bruised, yet alive,
rests on slimy wall,
reproduces,
finally
breaks *you* down.

BUSY FLOATING, THANK YOU

My head is stuffed
goopy water gushes
like a flooded creek
after a long rain.

My ears are jammed
with air and gunk. A dam
blocks sound so well
I can't hear.

My body separates
at my neck. I'm in a pool
of mud, so deep
I can't get air.

My lungs noisily wrack
from deep within,
gather garbage in my throat
to spit, not swallow.

Forehead burns palms,
sheens with sweat,
cheeks are cherries. So tired,
must have run a marathon.

Would go to work
but I'm busy floating.

TIME MACHINE

My nose contains
a wondrous time machine
rushes me between tenses
and faraway places.
My nose is
calibrated to detect
aromas triggering memories.

Odors sweet, foul
lick my nostrils,
descend onto tiny nodes,
while some creep
down my throat
to wake my tongue.
Smells become taste
two senses one.

SIX BILLION YEARS

I screamed, bare butt
on cold metal tray,
like an early morning fog
adrift, an incoherent
mass of drops.
Fresh from nothing,
fresh from the dead,
my heart beat blood
from brain to toes.

One day, young and small,
a screen of vision, smell,
sight, hearing, touch
flickered on, off, on, off
until awake and aware,
no longer unconscious,
no longer in land of dead.

I played, laughed, cried, sang,
enjoyed others' senses,
words, misdeeds, kindnesses.
I lived hard, softly, quickly,
gently as if deftly stroked
with purpose and strength
onto an oil painting
with a new horsehair brush.

Someday I lie down,
to return to long cycle
of inorganic, organic pools.
Six billion years
with the dead,
eighty like the flash
of a camera to illuminate,
capture moments, observe,
then with certainty journey
another six billion.

RENDERER

A steely screech
clangs off canyon walls.
Black silhouette slices
across searing sphere
to race atop
ground, grass.

His face, Death's masque,
with scimitar beak.
Eyes in the sky
calculate how many
will end skewered
with dual epees.

Scarlet blood
in daily ritual
baptizes
loamy earth,
paints grass
red, purple, black.

His form flows,
cruises in circles,
dives, transforms
into a ripper
that rives,
renders doom.

NEW FLOWER

Through taxi window
high plateau people
surly, busy, are watching.
Many, charred from purple rays
wear t-shirts with failed slogans, dirty denims,
linen dresses, bourkas, threadbare,
holy from hard, heavy labor,
scatter across road's narrow shoulders.
Taxis, cars, buses, lorries
pirouette like thousands of dancers
compete, deliver imported beer,
clothes, rebar, concrete, sand
riders disembark, transform
into more road people.

Like weeds in neglected gardens
buildings in all stages of morphology
thrust up high and low
threaten view of world's edge.
Finished ones shiny, erect, patient.
Many have wood pole scaffolding
pieced together with sweat, blood,
others are grey skeletons wait for flesh.
Offices, businesses, hotels
proliferate like children,
children of children.

Dishes dot roofs of rich,
some not, fill sets, screens
until invisible beams
deliver shows, movies, sitcoms,
news from Al-Jazeera, CNN,
camel races from Dubai.

With a hundred eyes, portals
they sanguinely stare
at fellow brothers, sisters
while inside moderns dream
just as in royal days
of a working toilet,
a treat to treasure.

DELIVERED

I slide across veins
of green grainy oak leaves,
move across their thin edges,
bend a frail point back,
sense slick textures
that turn light to food.

I glide through a forest
of oak, sycamore, maple, elm.
Breezes born in branches above
cool my face, neck, arms,
flickering sunbeams cascade
across my upturned eyes.

Hard, flaky, rippled barks
roughen my spread palm
while trunks sway back and forth
just behind meadow's edge.
Wind whishes through treetops,
while leaves loosen, fly.

I emerge from the forest,
into the green flow
of a raging river of grass.

CASUAL CHOICE

Snowflakes fall in torrents
tumble down tinted windows
as I shiver inside their black behemoth.
Watch passing pristine covered road,
we cut into Lucky's Pine Barrens.

The tires crunch snow and ice
like this thug who crushes walnuts
in his fingers as if they were my bones,
maybe my balls, maybe both.
Suddenly we slowly stop at a fork.

Yanked outside the obsidian monster
I am knelt before two roads,
one left, one right, winding their ways
into invisible white, cold dark.
Years ago, I chose a direction.

Only now do I know,
with knees sliced by ice and snow,
what that casual choice meant.
Odd, an old man sits in a horse-drawn cart
under a laden bough. He waits for me.

TW (Tim) Williams has been a bartender, sanitarian, teacher, Peace Corps Volunteer and an industrial hygienist. He is always a poet. His poems have been published in literary magazines including *The Alembic, The Griffin, Diverse Voices, The Dos Passos Review and others* in the last six years. One of his poems, "Her Callipygian Behind", won tenth place in the *Writer's Digest*'s 6th Poetry Competition.

CPSIA information can be obtained
at www.ICGtesting.com
Printed in the USA
LVHW03s1543020718
582500LV00039B/1474/P